Smoothies & Juices

By Ed Marquand
Photography by Marsha Burns

Smoothies
& Juices

Abbeville Press   Publishers
New York   London

Text copyright © 1998 Marquand Books, Inc. Images © 1998
Marsha Burns except jacket front and back and pages 3–5,
10–13, 16, 19, 20 bottom, 21, 23, 26, 36, 50, 52, 64–68, 73,
78–81 © 1998 Ed Marquand. Compilation, including selection
of text and images, copyright © 1998 Abbeville Press and
Marquand Books, Inc. All rights reserved under international
copyright conventions. No part of this book may be repro-
duced or utilized in any form or by any means, electronic or
mechanical, including photocopying, recording, or by any
information storage and retrieval system, without permission
in writing from the publisher. Inquiries should be addressed to
Abbeville Publishing Group, 116 West 23rd Street, New York,
NY 10011. The text of this book was set in Officina Sans with
display type in Arta.
Printed in Hong Kong.

First edition
10 9 8 7 6 5

Library of Congress Cataloging-in-Publication Data
Marquand, Ed.
    Smoothies & juices / by Ed Marquand ; photographs by
Marsha Burns.—1st ed.
    Includes index.
    ISBN 0-7892-0350-2
    1. Fruit juices. 2. Vegetable juices. I. Title.
TX811.M38 1998
641.8'75—dc21   97-39200

Please note: All recipes in *Smoothies & Juices* have been tested
to be safe. However, always consult with your physician if you
have any doubts or if you have a medical condition or any al-
lergies. If you are diabetic or suffer from gout or hypoglycemia,
check with your physician before drinking straight fruit juice.
Papaya can cause an adverse reaction in persons taking certain
antidepressants or antihypertensives. Author and publisher ac-
cept no liability with regard to the use of the recipes contained
in this book.

Designed by Ed Marquand with assistance by Melanie Milkie
Edited by Meredith Wolf Schizer and Marie Weiler
Produced by Marquand Books, Inc.

Jacket/cover front: *Orange, Pomegranate* juice (page 37)
Jacket/cover back: *Carrot, Beet, Ginger* juice (page 51)
Half title page: *Grapefruit, Banana, Cantaloupe* juice
(page 37)
Frontispiece: Strawberry and lemon juice (left) and
watermelon and lime juice (right)
Title page: Blueberry, blackberry, and lemon juice
Pages 4–5: *Pineapple, Tangerine, Banana* smoothie
(page 43)

Contents

Introduction

Smoothies and juices are not only wonderfully delicious but make good nutrition sense for active men, women, and children. Quick and simple to prepare, they require only easy-to-find ingredients and a minimum of equipment. You may discover that these delicious drinks are the most efficient way for you to take control of your nutritional and dietary intake, allowing you to maintain balance and stability in your eating habits.

What makes a smoothie different from a juice? For the purpose of this book, juices consist of the fluids and solids extracted from fruits and vegetables. Juices can be cold, room temperature, or warm. Smoothies, on the other hand, are always cool or cold, are mixed in a blender, and usually consist of a thickener, or binding element—like dairy or soy milk, yogurt, ice cream, sorbet, gelato, banana, or just plain ice—added to a base of fruit juice. Think of smoothies as power milkshakes for quick starts, stamina, and soothing refreshment. As a snack, quick meal, or side beverage to a light lunch, smoothies can't be beat.

Celery, Grapefruit juice (page 61)

Milkshakes without guilt. Unlike conventional milkshakes, smoothies do not need to be high in calories or fat. As you try some of the recipes in this book, experiment with the amount of milk, yogurt, or ice cream you put into your drink. You may be surprised by how little you need to soften and mellow the taste of the fruit juice. Most of the recipes here are delicious with the addition of just nonfat plain yogurt, an excellent source of protein and calcium without fat.

Don't forget flavor. This book isn't just about grabbing a fast meal in a glass—it's about experiencing and enjoying bold flavors and rich textures in refreshing, rejuvenating concoctions. By distilling and concentrating flavor, juicing reveals nuances of flavor that cooking often dulls or even destroys. Also, the possible combinations of fruits and vegetables are almost endless: modern growing, shipping, and storing techniques have made it possible to savor delectable and exotic tropical fruits or summery herbs and vegetables all year long, with a different treat almost every day.

Vegetable cocktails and juice soups. Don't stop with simple summer drinks. With a little more thought and preparation you can heat delicious vegetable cocktails to make soothing, warming

Cold tomato and lemon juice with
yogurt and spinach garnish

soups. You can take these in a thermos to the office or the ski slope for additional enjoyment. Leftover vegetable juices can be used as soup bases.

Good-bye to food fights. Smoothies are an excellent way to make sure the kids are getting proper nutrients too. Since texture and appearance affect a youngster's enthusiasm for unpopular foods and since most kids love milkshakes, you may be able to get yours to drink what they won't eat. You may have to do a sleight of hand at the mixer, but it's worth a try.

Preparation. The recipes here are organized by basic ingredient. For many of them you can decide whether you want to concoct a terrific juice or a refreshing smoothie by making slight adjustments in the preparation. When both forms are possible, preparation advice is offered. Serving sizes vary, but generally, a small serving is approximately one cup (240 ml); a medium serving, one and a half cups (360 ml); and a large serving, two cups (480 ml). Blenders whip air into a beverage, and some ingredients create froth, so use these measures as general guidelines only.

Juices for health, diet, and weight maintenance. Pills may have their place, but juices provide a better means of ingesting the vitamins, minerals, and trace elements so vital to your health

Left: Banana and orange smoothie
Above: *Orange, Apple, Ginger* juice (page 37)

and your immune system. This book makes no claim to prevent or cure any of the array of health maladies that confront us, but it gives recipes for making tasty drinks that are good for you, and any doctor or nutritionist will tell you that eating properly is essential to enjoying and preserving good health and to maintaining your ideal weight. This book will present you with quick and efficient ways to meet your nutritional goals.

"Live" foods. Live foods are fresh, uncooked fruits and vegetables still teeming with vitamins, amino acids, and essential trace elements. The benefits of "live" foods are difficult to prove empirically but become obvious when you feel them boosting your energy level. The premise is simple: processing and cooking destroy much of the nutritional value of most of the food we eat. Even store-bought 100-percent juice has been processed to the point that most of the vitamins and minerals listed on the label are additives. The closer you stay to fresh-picked, ripe fruits and vegetables, the more nutritional benefits you reap. Make the juices described in this book from the freshest, most delicious ingredients you can find. This puts you—not some huge factory a thousand miles away—in charge of what you ingest.

What if I just eat the vegetables, instead of juicing them? Eating them is fine, but be prepared to do a lot of chewing. You would have to eat four or five cups (560–700 g) of chopped carrots or celery to equal the nutrients in one cup (240 ml) of carrot or celery juice. Juice gives

Above: Yogurt and blueberries

Left: Orange smoothie

you more than 90 percent of the nutrients from each ingredient, so you can see how much easier it is to drink rather than chew them. Also, while raw vegetables can take hours to digest, the nutrients in juice are absorbed more quickly and efficiently, so you feel the benefits right away.

Isn't bulk good? Certainly it is, and fiber is necessary for proper digestion; you *should* supplement your diet with bulk. Most fruit has lots of fiber and is easier to digest than most vegetables, so you may want to eat more fruit and drink more vegetables. Juice made in a blender

(as opposed to a juicer) retains all the original fiber, so with a good balance of fruit, fruit drinks, juice, raw or cooked vegetables, beans, and whole grains, you will be well supplied with essential vitamins, minerals, amino acids, and fiber. You can also save pulp from the juicer and use it in baking and soups (see page 21).

Some vitamins need fat to work. If you are dieting, resist the temptation to completely eliminate fat from your diet; you may be doing yourself harm in the process. Some vitamins, like B and E, are only soluble in your system with fat. It would be a shame to gulp down a vitamin-rich drink only to flush the nutrients through your system without giving them a chance to give you a boost! Simply adding a little low-fat milk or yogurt or eating a low-fat snack with your drink will do the trick.

One word of caution. If you are diabetic or suffer from gout or hypoglycemia, you should check with your physician before drinking straight fruit juice. The large quantity of natural sugar in fruit juice may be absorbed into your system too quickly and trigger a reaction.

Techniques

Pick the right technique.
Each type of ingredient behaves differently when it is juiced or shredded. Take a carrot or stalk of celery, for example, and run it through the juicer. You will extract a flavorful liquid concentrate of vitamins, minerals, amino acids, and trace elements. Open the cover and you will discover a high proportion of pulp left behind. Thus, juicing these base ingredients is the way to go.

Take a chunk of honeydew melon, cantaloupe, or peeled peach and slip that into the juicer chute. You will get a nice portion of juice but almost no pulp—virtually all the fruit has spun through the extraction filter. You could have blended the fruit in a blender or food processor with similar results and perhaps less cleanup.

So how do you decide which technique to use? If you plan to use carrots or celery as the base ingredient, the juicer is essential. As a general rule, if your ingredients are not pulpy, you should blend them. You can make some great fruit juices in the blender and drink all of the pulp with the juice. Some recipes that call for a variety of ingredients can be prepared most easily using both a juicer and a blender. Our recipes will help you select the best method for producing your drinks and give you ideas for concocting your own recipes.

What about herbs and small quantities of items? If you want to create your juice with a juicer but don't want to use two appliances, you can still add sprigs of herbs, bits of garlic, or small pieces of onion. Wrap them in a lettuce or cabbage leaf or sandwich them between two firm ingredients—between two celery stalks, for example. Or chop them finely and insert them in a cut in a tomato or apple before sending it down the chute.

Herbs and nuts may be easier to add by grinding

Clockwise from top: Celery juice, beet juice, and yogurt

Use your coffee grinder to grind fresh herbs to add to vegetable drinks.

Asparagus down the chute

them first. A coffee grinder works well for this, but if you are blending you may be able to just chop them in the blender before adding the main ingredients. Nuts and even nut butters can add an unexpected and rich taste and texture to the right smoothie.

Enhancing flavors by combining. Producers of fine wines have long known that mixing varieties of grapes is the best way to achieve a full-bodied flavor. But you don't need to be a vintner to make better, richer juice flavors by simple mixing. As you become more familiar with the principals of juicing, through the recipes in this book and your own experimentation, you will discover that fruit and vegetable flavors intensify when they're concentrated, but they also support one another when mixed with the right complements. A nectarine early in the season doesn't taste as good as one a month later. However, if you juice together an early nectarine with strawberries and blueberries, all of the flavors are enhanced.

Sequence can be important. You can make it easier and faster to clean the juicer by planning the order in which you insert the ingredients. Alternate hard and soft foods, and end with something hard;

Parsley adds a clean spark to your vegetable drinks.

Add soda water to your juice for a fizzy sparkle or add tonic water for a brisk, cooling curve.

the hard foods help push through the soft ones. Flavoring ingredients—like ginger, onion, and garlic—should be followed by base ingredients, to wash the strong flavors and odors away.

Simple cleanup. Juicing equipment is easier to clean than most food processors, and cleanup is especially easy if you rinse your appliance and utensils immediately after use and follow up later with a thorough washing in warm water. The pulp collection basket, however, will need to be cleaned more thoroughly, and a produce brush can help. Don't let food accumulate and dry in the juicer. After heavy use, you may want to soak the parts in a mild solution of vinegar and water. Then scrub each part clean, rinse, and dry thoroughly. Most of the better juicers have parts that are dishwasher safe. Some juicer manufacturers sell optional paper filters for clear juices that make for quicker cleanup.

Thinning with other liquids. Many fruits and vegetables do not create juice when processed but instead produce a syrup or pudding that must be thinned. If you're processing in a blender, add a little liquid to the blender, but if you're processing in a juicer, add liquid *after* the juice has been extracted. For a thinner, you can use mineral water or, for a fizzy sparkle, soda water. Tonic water throws a

Clean-up is easy if you rinse your juicer and blender parts immediately after each use. Use a small brush to clean the pulp collection basket.

Peaches (above) are very low in calories and make a smooth, mellow drink. Blackberries (below) are more tart and the hard, tiny seeds give your drink a grainy texture. Lemons give a piquant touch to any drink.

brisk, cooling curve to fruit tastes, and herbal teas result in especially tasty beverages when the combination works right. But don't over-thin; stir in a little liquid and add more until your drink is as light as you like it.

To skin or not to skin? If you would normally eat the skin of a fruit, it is okay to juice it. As a general rule, you can juice the rinds or skins of many organically grown fruits and vegetables, but if you suspect that the skins have been exposed to heavy doses of pesticides, play it safe and peel them off. Some vegetables, like cucumbers, are waxed to help preserve them and improve their appearance; you should peel these.

And the seeds? Big seeds and pits, like peach and cherry stones, should not go into your juicer or blender or into your drinks. Most melon seeds are easy to remove. Apple and pear seeds will be shredded in a juicer and caught by the pulp basket, but a blender will chew them into small but noticeable bits, so remove them first. Some berries are covered with hard, tiny seeds that though unnoticed in unprocessed fruit, add a gritty texture to a beverage. If this texture is likely to distract you from the pleasures of the drink, strain the juice with a wire mesh.

Particularly fibrous vegetables, like carrots, leave a pulp that makes an excellent textural additive for baked goods, soups, and broths.

Can juice be stored? It can, but of course it is better when fresh. Nutrients oxidize and do not last long when exposed to air, but if the question is whether to drink day-old juice or a diet soda, the answer should be obvious. You can store your juice in a chilled thermos and take it to work with you, but to cut down on oxidation and loss of nutri-ents, fill the thermos to the brim and try not to trap any air inside. At home, store extra juice in a thermos or some other airtight container and keep it in the refrigerator. Yes, it is a good idea to keep the thermos in the refrigerator too.

What to do with the pulp? Ingredients juiced in a juicer, particularly fibrous ones like carrots and celery, will leave a pulp that makes an excellent textural additive for baked goods, soups, and broths. If your juicer is highly efficient, it will extract most of the flavor; taste the pulp to see how much flavor remains. Depending on your recipes, you can put rich pulp to good use as extenders in cakes, breads, muffins, cookies, and tarts. Of course, each recipe is different, so experiment with small amounts of pulp and add more if you like the effect. One-half cup (115 g) of pulp kneaded into a loaf of bread is a good measure to experiment with. Heartier breads can take heftier doses. A few table-spoons stirred into a pie filling could provide good bulk. You can even freeze the pulp in small portions, defrosting before use. If it is unlikely you will use the pulp or if it is full of seeds and bits of inedible rind, pulp also makes great fodder for composting.

Apple-based Drinks

Even by itself, fresh apple juice is a delicious and refreshing drink. Mix in other fruits to make it memorable. Consider the following combinations as starting points and be sure to experiment with different varieties of apples. Whether Gala, Granny Smith, or Fuji is your current favorite or the tastiest pick of the season, give it a spin in your juicer; then blend in other fruits to suit your mood. Any of the recipes in this section can be created in a juicer or in a blender.

Juicer suggestions: Firm fruit will give you more clear and pure juice. You don't need to seed or peel apples, but do remove the stem and flower at the base. A medium-size apple should yield about ½ cup (120 ml) of juice. If you plan to juice ginger, berries, or kiwifruit, first juice a few apple wedges, follow with the softer ingredients, and finish up with the rest of the apples. Sandwich mint leaves between two apple wedges before inserting them into the juicer chute. As an alternative, you can process the softer items in the blender and then add the apple juice after the other ingredients have reached a smooth consistency. Pomegranate juice is much more easily extracted in a juicer.

Left: *Apple, Mango, Ginger* juice (page 27)

Blender suggestions: Mix softer apples in the blender. Remove the seeds, stem, and flower, and peel if you prefer. Chop into 1-inch (2.5 cm) cubes and pulse the blender at the slowest speed until the fruit breaks up and liquefies. Leave the blender running until the juice is your desired consistency.

Ginger can be minced and dropped into a blender first with a bit of apple. Blend until the ginger is very fine—stopping occasionally to push down the pieces with a rubber spatula—and then add the other ingredients.

Smoothie options: Ice, sorbet, or ice cream (½ cup/120 ml) should be dropped into the blender after the juice is mixed. You can add milk or yogurt to the blender, or you can whisk it in by hand. Remember that lemon juice curdles milk, so adjust your recipe accordingly.

Warm juices: Warm apple-based juices are delicious. Heat gently in a saucepan until warm. Do not boil.

Apple, Lemon, Ginger juice (page 26)

Apple, Pomegranate juice

tangy Apple, Lemon, Ginger

1 medium apple
½ lemon, yellow skin removed but pith retained
1 cherry-size button ginger, peeled

Process and mix.

Makes one small serving

sunny Apple, Cherry, Lemon

1 medium apple
12 cherries, pitted
½ lemon, yellow skin removed but pith retained

Process and mix.

Makes one small serving

snappy Apple, Strawberry, Banana, Mint

3 small sprigs mint
6 strawberries, tops removed
1 banana, peeled
1 medium apple, cut in wedges

Put two sprigs of the mint in the blender with 2 tablespoons water and blend until the mint is ground. Then add separately the strawberries, banana, and apple wedges. Blend to a uniform consistency. Garnish with the remaining mint sprig.

Makes one small serving

summery Apple, Cherry, Strawberry

1 medium apple
12 cherries, pitted
6 strawberries

Process and mix.

Makes one medium serving

puckery Apple, Pomegranate

1 medium apple
½ cup (85 g) pomegranate seeds

Process in a juicer and mix.

Makes one medium serving

Warmed Apple, Pear, Nutmeg, Cinnamon

1 medium apple
1 firm pear
pinch nutmeg
pinch cinnamon

Process and mix. Warm in a saucepan but do not boil.

Makes one medium serving

Warmed Apple, Pear, Nutmeg, Cinnamon juice

Apple, Cranberry, Blueberry

1 medium apple
¼ cup (25 g) cranberries
½ cup (70 g) blueberries

Process and mix. Warm in a saucepan but do not boil.

Makes one medium serving

Apple, Mango, Ginger

1 medium apple
1 mango, peeled and pitted
1 cherry-size button ginger, peeled

Process and mix.

Makes one medium serving

Pear-based Drinks

Have you ever found a pear that looked delectable, but when you bit into it, it was just a little too hard? That's the perfect level of ripeness for putting pears through the juicer. On the other hand, pears that are a little overripe but still taste sweet process better in the blender. Run them through with or without the skin; remove the seeds and stem.

Pears oxidize and turn dark when exposed to air, and so does the juice, so don't let it sit around for long.

Smoothie options: Since they're so sweet, pears make a good base for unsweetened yogurt smoothies. Just add ½ cup (120 ml) of plain yogurt to any of these drinks.

bumptious Pear, Apple, Cranberry, Cinnamon

1 medium pear
1 medium apple
½ cup (45 g) cranberries
pinch cinnamon

Process and mix.

Makes one small serving

saucy Pear, Grape, Cranberry

1 medium pear
1 cup (150 g) seedless grapes, red or green
½ cup (45 g) cranberries

Process and mix.

Makes one serving

sassy Pear, Apple, Nectarine

1 medium pear
1 medium apple
1 medium nectarine

Process and mix.

Makes one large serving

Pear, Grape, Cranberry juice

Melon-based Drinks

In season, melon drinks are unexpectedly delicious. Ripe melons are necessary, and since so little fiber is captured in the juicer's spinner basket, it's easiest to mix these recipes in a blender. Cantaloupe and honeydew are easy to seed, and if you slice them right, even watermelons can be easy to seed. Cut the watermelon in half lengthwise, then cut each of the halves lengthwise again. The core will be free of seeds; slice it out to use for juicing. Then spoon out the seed layer and you are left with relatively seed-free fruit. Slice the fruit free of the rind and process. Once extracted, melon juice separates quickly, so serve it with a swizzle stick or spoon.

The usual smoothie ingredients work here; try ½ cup (120 ml) of plain or vanilla yogurt, ice cream, or sorbet.

Melon juices

delightful Honeydew, Strawberry, Mint

6 strawberries
1 sprig mint
½ medium honeydew

Process the strawberries and mint until the leaves are thoroughly chopped. Add melon.

Makes one medium serving

Watermelon juice

zesty Watermelon, Lime, Mint

1 lime
1 sprig mint
¼ medium watermelon

Process the lime and mint until the leaves are thoroughly chopped. Add watermelon.

Makes one medium serving

bright Watermelon, Cantaloupe, Honeydew

¼ medium watermelon
¼ cantaloupe
¼ honeydew

Process.

Makes one large serving

buoyant Honeydew spritzer

½ medium honeydew melon
1 cup (240 ml) very cold
    sparkling water
1 small sprig mint

Process the melon. Pour the juice
into a glass and add the spar-
kling water. Mix by hand. Serve
with mint leaves as garnish.

Makes one large serving

Citrus-based Drinks

Bottled or reconstituted citrus juices don't compare to the dazzling taste of fresh-squeezed. And fresh juice gets even better when you add other flavors. Many of the recipes in this section are made with ingredients that don't require a power juicer. Instructions call for either a blender alone or a reamer juicer for the citrus ingredients and a blender for the other ingredients, although pomegranate juice is best extracted with a juicer. Citrus juices produced in a reamer are clear. Blended citrus juices are pulpier.

Pick citrus fruit that is ripe and heavy. Smaller oranges and grape-fruits are usually juicier. And don't overlook limes; compared to lem-ons, they are usually juicier and sweeter and have fewer seeds. During the winter, mandarin oranges, or satsumas, are plentiful and delicious. Peel all citrus fruits before processing.

Kiwifruit and bananas should also be peeled, as should mangoes and papaya, which also need to be pitted.

These drinks all make excellent smoothies. Just add ½ cup (120 ml) thickener (yogurt, ice cream, or sorbet) in the final mo-ments of blending.

A word of caution: Papaya can cause problems for persons taking certain antidepressants or antihypertensives. Check with your physi-cian if you have any doubts.

Like lemons, limes add tartness to both fruit and vegetable drinks.

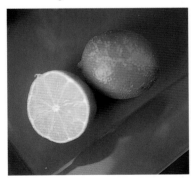

Orange, Grape, Pear juice (page 37)

delectable Orange, Grape, Pear

3 medium oranges

1 handful seedless grapes, green or red

1 pear

Blend until liquified.

Makes one large serving

succulent Orange, Pomegranate

4 medium oranges

¼ cup (40 g) pomegranate seeds

Process in a juicer.

Makes one medium serving

alluring Warmed Mandarin Orange, Ginger, Honey

6 mandarin oranges (satsumas) peeled

1 teaspoon finely grated fresh ginger

1 teaspoon honey

Juice oranges. Gently heat juice over low heat. Add ginger and honey. Warm to desired temperature.

Makes one medium serving

Exotic emerald satsumas make a tasty variation in citrus drinks.

pert Orange, Apple, Ginger

3 medium oranges

1 medium apple

1 teaspoon finely grated fresh ginger

Blend oranges until liquified. Add chunks of apple and ginger.

Makes one large serving

luscious Grapefruit, Banana, Cantaloupe

1 medium grapefruit

1 banana

¼ cantaloupe

Mix in a blender.

Makes one large serving

Orange, Pomegranate juice

Like other tropical fruit, kiwifruit make a perfect complement to citrus fruits.

gregarious Grapefruit, Celery, Tangerine, Orange, Mango

1 medium grapefruit
5 stalks celery
1 medium tangerine
1 medium orange
1 mango

Mix in a blender.

Makes one large serving

lusty Orange, Mango, Papaya

2 oranges
1 mango
1 papaya

Mix in a blender.

Makes one large serving

tantalizing Orange, Pineapple, Kiwifruit

2 oranges
¼ pineapple
2 kiwifruit

Mix in a blender.

Makes one large serving

impetuous Orange, Banana, Lime

2 oranges
1 banana, peeled
1 lime

Mix in a blender.

Makes one large serving

Add a touch of lemon to any non-citrus drink to keep it from turning brown.

Tropical Drinks

Since so many tropical fruits turn to purée in a juicer, prepare these recipes in a blender. It's easier all around, especially if the fruit is good and ripe. You may need to add small amounts of liquid to help the blender do its job. Add ¼ cup (60 ml) of water, juice, or other liquid at a time. For a tasty smoothie add crushed ice, milk, yogurt, ice cream, or sorbet to suit your mood. Stir in ½ cup (120 ml) of your choice after the fruit is blended.

Pineapples should be peeled and cubed. Use the tougher core if you like your juice chewier. Peel citrus fruits and bananas as well as mangoes and papaya, which should also be pitted.

snappy Pineapple, Apple

¼ pineapple

1 apple

Blend to desired consistency.

Makes one large serving

daring Pineapple, Mango

¼ pineapple

1 mango

Blend to desired consistency.

Makes one large serving

Left: The smooth, meaty texture and mellow flavors of most tropical fruits make them ideal candidates for smoothies.

Right: Mangoes have a rich, buttery flavor.

41

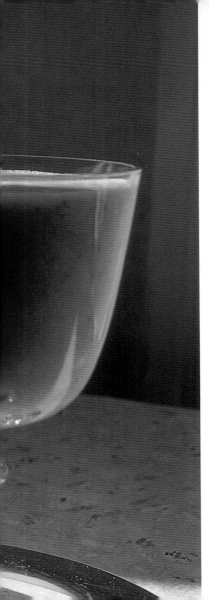

exotic Pineapple, Tangerine, Banana

¼ pineapple

3 tangerines

1 banana

Blend to desired consistency.

Makes one large serving

provocative Blood Orange, Banana

6 blood oranges

1 banana

Blend to desired consistency.

Makes one large serving

spunky Lime, Papaya, Honey

4 limes

1 papaya

1 tablespoon honey

Blend to desired consistency.

Makes one medium serving

passionate Grapefruit, Mango, Banana

1 grapefruit

1 mango

1 teaspoon honey

1 banana

Blend to desired consistency.

Makes one large serving

Left to right:
Pineapple, Mango
juice (page 41);
*Grapefruit, Mango,
Banana* juice;
Strawberry, pine-
apple smoothie

Berry and Stone Fruit—based Drinks

Most berries make excellent juice and smoothie ingredients, but some, like blackberries, have hard, tiny seeds that some people find distasteful. Blackberry juice can be delectable, so if the seeds don't bother you, you can add or substitute blackberries for the blueberries in the following recipes. Strawberries and raspberries are also delicious and easy-to-use ingredients. Fresh or frozen, their flavor provides a refreshing zing to these drinks.

Stone fruit is easy to work with as well. Peel the peaches if you prefer or use nectarines instead. Remove all pits. You can add figs, apricots, or prunes to these drinks, but if you do add dried fruit, soften it in warm water or juice for an hour or so before adding it to the blender.

All these recipes can be made in a blender more easily than in a juicer. Adding ½ cup (120 ml) yogurt or your favorite smoothie ingredient mellows any of these concoctions.

Left and above: Watermelon and lemon juice and strawberry and lemon juice

inspiring Strawberry, Orange, Blueberry

2 cups (300 g) strawberries
1 medium orange
1 cup (140 g) blueberries

Blend to desired consistency.

Makes one large serving

zingy Strawberry, Blueberry, Raspberry, Apple

2 cups (300 g) strawberries
½ cup (70 g) blueberries
½ cup (65 g) raspberries
1 apple

Blend to desired consistency.

Makes one large serving

tempting Peach, Strawberry, Apple

1 medium peach
1 cup (150 g) strawberries
1 medium apple

Blend to desired consistency.

Makes one medium serving

Left: *Plum, Peach, Blueberry* juice
(page 47)

Above: Mango purée and blueberries

Opposite: Strawberry smoothie served
as a soup

intriguing Mango, Blueberry, Apple

1 mango

1 cup (140 g) blueberries

1 apple

Blend to desired consistency.

Makes one medium serving

demure Nectarine, Strawberry, Blueberry

1 nectarine

1 cup (150 g) strawberries

1 cup (140 g) blueberries

Blend to desired consistency.

Makes one medium serving

heavenly Plum, Peach, Blueberry

3 plums

1 peach

1 cup (140 g) blueberries

Blend to desired consistency.

Makes one medium serving

enchanting Apricot, Plum, Apple

5 fresh apricots

3 plums

1 apple

Blend to desired consistency.

Makes one medium serving

balmy Apricot, Pear, Plum

5 fresh apricots

1 pear

3 plums

Blend to desired consistency.

Makes one medium serving

Vegetable Juice Recipes

If you include a strong flavor, like garlic, onion, or basil, begin the sequence of juicing with a portion of the base ingredient. Follow with the strongest flavors; then "clean" your juicer by finishing with the remaining base ingredient. You will still need to rinse the exposed parts of the juicer with warm water and scrub the traps and filters with a produce brush, but most of the strong odor will be eliminated by the base flavor.

Ingredients with strong flavor need to handled with care. Experiment by catching their juices in a separate glass, and then mix them into the base juice a little at a time until you find the right proportion for your taste. Beets are powerful, and you should try them in smaller doses to start. The same is true for jalapeño, ginger, garlic, onion, parsley, fennel, and basil. Conversely, celery juice has a mild, neutral flavor and makes a good base for juices with strong flavors.

Bell peppers make zesty juice additives, especially the red, yellow, or orange ones.

Vegetable smoothies: Although most smoothies are fruit based, any of the vegetable drinks taste great with a little unflavored, unsweetened yogurt, and this is a quick and delicious way to add protein and calcium to your beverage. Start with ¼ cup (60 ml) and add more as desired.

Warmed vegetable cocktails: Can you drink vegetable soup from a cup? Sure. And you can warm juice on cold winter days also. Heat it through without boiling, to retain most of the nutrients.

Carrot, Tomato, Jalapeño juice (page 53)

Carrot-based Drinks

A crunchy carrot makes a tasty, wholesome snack, but the flavor of fresh carrot juice can be astonishingly satisfying. The difference is in the high ratio of pulp to juice; remove the pulp and you have concentrated, sweet flavor. It takes ten big, fat carrots to produce about 2½ cups (360 ml) of juice. But that's a lot of carrot flavor; after experimenting you may decide that you prefer diluting carrot juice with celery or apple. (Or perhaps you *will* want it all!)

robust Carrot, Beet, Ginger

5 medium carrots
¼ beet
1 cherry-size button ginger, peeled

Juice two carrots. Add the beet and ginger.
Follow with the remaining carrots.

Makes one medium serving

Carrot, Beet, Ginger juice

restorative Carrot, Beet, Spinach

5 medium carrots

¼ beet

1 big handful fresh spinach leaves,
carefully rinsed

Juice two carrots. Add the beet and spinach.
Follow with the remaining carrots.

Makes one medium serving

piquant Carrot, Tomato, Jalapeño

5 medium carrots

3 medium tomatoes

½ jalapeño, seeded

Juice two carrots. Add the tomatoes and jalapeño.
Follow with the remaining carrots.

Makes one medium serving

vigorous Carrot, Celery, Apple

5 medium carrots

5 celery stalks

1 medium apple

Juice two carrots. Add the celery and apple. Follow
with the remaining carrots.

Makes one large serving

Carrot juice is loaded with flavor and can
be astonishingly satisfying.

Tomato-based Drinks

Canned tomato juice, which looks like watered-down ketchup, bears little resemblance to the fresh version, which is surprisingly light and refreshing. Although technically a fruit, tomatoes work best with other vegetables. You don't need to skin or seed tomatoes if you don't want to, and ripe tomatoes process better in the blender unless you're mixing them with celery, spinach, asparagus, or other fibrous ingredients. If you prefer tomato juice without skin and seeds, strain the juice after blending.

With all the varieties of tomatoes available today, be sure to select the kind with the most flavor, and don't overlook cherry tomatoes, since each one packs a lot of taste.

tangy Tomato, Bell Pepper, Asparagus

1 bell pepper, seeded with stem removed

1 large ripe beefsteak tomato or 1 cup (165 g) cherry tomatoes

5 medium asparagus spears

Process half of the bell pepper. Follow with the tomato, then the asparagus. Finish with remaining bell pepper.

Makes one medium serving

savory Tomato, Spinach, Onion

1 large, ripe beefsteak tomato or 2 cups (320 g) cherry tomatoes

1 large handful fresh spinach leaves, carefully rinsed

¼ small yellow, white, or red onion

Process half of the tomatoes. Follow with the spinach and onion. Finish with remaining tomato.

Makes one medium serving

Tomato, Bell Pepper, Asparagus juice

Tomato, Basil, Onion, Garlic

2 medium tomatoes
several stems fresh basil, chopped
¼ medium onion, chopped
1 garlic clove, peeled

Process in a blender by starting with one tomato, then add the basil and onion. Extract the garlic juice with a garlic press. When the mixture liquefies, add the second tomato.

Makes one large serving

invigorating ## Tomato, Parsley, Bell Pepper

2 medium tomatoes
1 cup (15 g) loosely packed parsley with stems
1 bell pepper, seeded with stem removed

Process in a blender by starting with one tomato; then add the parsley. When thoroughly blended, add the pepper, then the second tomato.

Makes one large serving

peppy ## Tomato, Cucumber, Tabasco

2 medium tomatoes
1 cucumber, chopped
1 squirt Tabasco sauce

Process in a blender. Start with one tomato, then add the cucumber. When the mixture liquefies, add the second tomato and the Tabasco sauce.

Makes one large serving

titillating ## Tomato, Celery, Bell Pepper

4 stalks celery with leaves
1 large ripe beefsteak tomato or
1 cup (165 g) cherry tomatoes
1 bell pepper, preferably red, orange, or yellow, seeded with stem removed

If juicing, process two stalks of celery first, followed by the tomato and pepper; then finish with the last two celery stalks.

Makes one large serving

Celery, (red) bell pepper, and tomato juices, components of *Tomato, Celery, Bell Pepper*

Celery-based Drinks

Celery is subtle, so it makes a delightful and refreshing backdrop for stronger flavors. One bunch of celery produces about two cups (480 ml) of juice. Insert stalks leaf end first into the juicer chute. As with other fibrous ingredients, start and end with celery stalks to help clean the machine. If you are not using an entire bunch at one time, cut the bunch lengthwise to get a good mix of the heartier outside stalks and the more tender inside stalks, or heart. Lemon juice can help give celery some zing if it tastes a little too "green" for your mood.

racy Celery, Beet, Ginger

½ bunch celery

¼ beet

1 cherry-size button ginger, peeled

Juice half of the celery. Add beet and ginger. Follow with remaining celery.

Makes one medium serving

peppery Celery, Watercress, Radish, Lemon

½ bunch celery

¼ cup packed watercress

3 radishes

juice of ½ lemon

Juice half of the celery. Add watercress and radishes. Follow with remaining celery. Stir in lemon juice.

Makes one medium serving

Beet and celery juices, components of *Celery, Beet, Ginger*

Celery, Fennel, Cucumber

½ bunch celery

¼ bunch fennel

1 cucumber, quartered lengthwise

Juice half of the celery. Add fennel and cucumber. Follow with remaining celery.

Note: Fennel is not as strong as it smells, but still, a little can go a long way. A squirt of lemon or lime juice puts a zesty spin on this drink.

Makes one large serving

demure ## Celery, Asparagus, Lemon

½ bunch celery

5 asparagus spears

½ lemon, yellow skin removed but pith retained

Juice half of the celery. Add asparagus and lemon. Follow with remaining celery.

Makes one large serving

pert ## Celery, Red Bell Pepper, Lemon

½ bunch celery

1 red bell pepper, seeded with stem removed

½ lemon, yellow skin removed but pith retained

Juice half of the celery. Add pepper and lemon. Follow with remaining celery.

Makes one medium serving

refreshing ## Celery, Grapefruit

½ bunch celery

1 grapefruit, skinned

Juice half of the celery. Add grapefruit. Follow with remaining celery.

Makes one large serving

Celery, Fennel, Cucumber juice (left) and *Celery, Watercress, Radish, Lemon* juice (right; page 59)

Basic Equipment

Citrus juicers. Because they are hand operated, citrus juicers, also called reamers and press juicers, are quite inexpensive. Simple hand pressure forces the juice out of its skin and into a glass or pitcher. This juice retains the pulp but not the pith—the white skin that surrounds citrus sections—which, by the way, is loaded with nutrients. If you want the benefit of those nutrients, peel the fruit, retaining as much of the pith as possible, and process in the blender. Chewy texture and more nutrients or a smooth texture with fewer? It's your choice.

Centrifugal juicers. Electric juicers are more elaborate than hand-operated ones, but most work on the same principal: as the ingredients are dropped into a chute, a fine blade inside a spinning basket shreds them; the basket holds the pulp and centrifugally dispenses the juice. It works much like a clothes-washing machine on the spin cycle, intensely extracting the juice. Some juicers have reamer attachments for citrus juicing. Generally, centrifugal juicers shred to a very fine and uniform texture.

Masticating juicers. These professional-grade juicers use high-pressure screws to wring juice out of fruits and vegetables. They can be highly efficient at squeezing flavor and nutrients from your ingredients, but they are slower, more expensive, and harder to clean.

Where to find them. Juicers are commonly sold in kitchen, appliance, and department stores and by mail order. Research current models and select an appliance that suits your lifestyle and that you will use regularly. There is a range of models to suit most budgets and anticipated uses. High-end professional juicers can run up to $1,000 plus attachments, but excellent-quality home juicers run in the $200 range, and some lower-priced models can be purchased for under $100.

This high-quality juicer will last for many years. The inside grinding blade and basket are made of stainless steel.

Blenders. Blenders are more basic than juicers and have many important advantages: They are quick to use and easy to clean; they can produce a greater variety of beverages; and they can grind ice. Rotating high-speed double blades at the bottom of a sturdy glass, plastic, or metal container quickly shred, pulverize, and eventually liquefy fruits and vegetables. Some models feature a variety of speeds and blade actions, but a sturdy basic blender will work just fine for all the recipes in this book. Models with a variety of speeds offer more textural options, but that is not essential to the preparation of fine juices and smoothies. A good blender can be purchased for well under $100.

With a blender you can control the texture of your drink by pulsing the motor and adjusting the running time, whereas with a juicer you will invariably end up with a uniformly fine texture. If you like the look and feel of chunks of fruits and vegetables in your juice, use a blender.

A clever cook can also figure out how to juice in a food processor, but they are not recommended since food processors were not designed for this.

Other equipment. The following utensils are helpful in juicing and making smoothies:

- small scrub brush for cleaning produce
- vegetable peeler
- small knife for coring
- large knife for chopping ingredients into a size your juicer chute or blender can handle efficiently
- rubber spatula for cleaning the sides of the blender or for pouring thick juice into a glass
- mesh strainer for filtering out seeds and chunks of pulp
- measuring cup to keep track of how much juice you've extracted

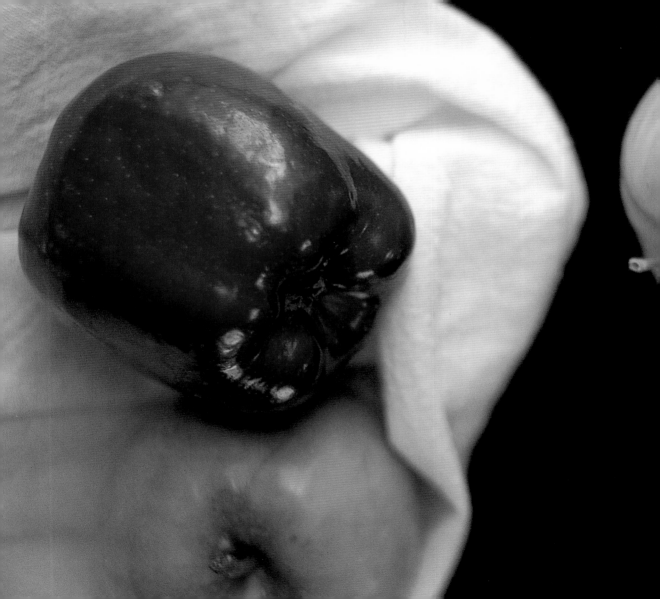

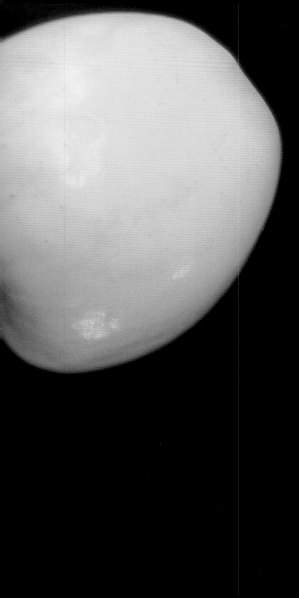

Shopping for and Storing the Basic Ingredients

The basic approach to juicing is simple. For most juices, start with a base ingredient that is high in moisture, then for additional flavor, texture, and nutrition add secondary ingredients that are drier. The most popular base ingredients are apple, pear, melons, citrus fruits, pineapple, berries, stone fruits, carrot, tomato, and celery. In general, mix fruits with fruits and vegetables with vegetables. Apples, however, make a fine accompaniment to most vegetables.

Fruit varieties seem to increase each year, so enjoy discovering the distinctions. Most apple juice can be described as fresh, sweet, and sharp, but that's just the beginning. Experiment with the various types: Granny Smith apples are much more tart than Delicious, for example, and Fujis, Braeburns, Winesaps, and Galas all produce terrific juice. Try each one and decide for yourself which you like best.

If there is a single surprise to novice juicers it is carrot juice. This valuable base ingredient is far sweeter than most people expect. And you do not need to be too fussy about carrots. While delicate baby French carrots taste wonderful whether raw or cooked, they may be too expensive for heavy-duty juicing. Their main appeal is their delicate texture, and since you are going to pulverize them in the juicer, stick to medium and large carrots that have lots of flavor but are not woody or dried out.

It is especially important that you select fresh and flavorful base ingredients. A stale and pulpy apple does not improve when it is juiced. Fortunately, most of the base ingredients used here are hardy and store well under proper conditions.

Shopping for produce. Use the same criteria to buy produce for juicing as you do for eating. Fruits and vegetables with the best flavor and substance are those that are in season and are ripe. They do not need to look 100 percent perfect; a bump or bruise will not affect the flavor, but produce at its peak will yield the best-tasting juice. Old, beat-up, limp fruits and vegetables belong in a compost pile.

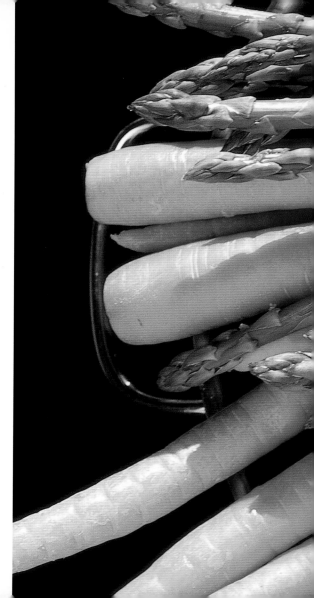

Should you use organic produce? This is entirely personal preference. If you normally shop for organic vegetables for cooking, you'll undoubtedly want to buy organic for juicing. Regardless, you should wash your produce gently but carefully with warm water. If you plan to juice the skins of fruits or vegetables that have been waxed, like apples and tomatoes, wash them with a mild soap or produce wash to remove residue. Beware of imported fruit from countries with more relaxed pesticide standards, and when in doubt, peel.

Storing produce. Leafy vegetables, like spinach, lettuce, watercress, and parsley, should be washed as soon as you get them home. Then dry thoroughly in a spinner and store in tight plastic bags in the refrigerator. Berries and root vegetables should also be stored in the refrigerator. Store tomatoes, apples, citrus fruits, stone fruits, peppers, tropical fruits, bananas, and ginger at room temperature. Keep ripe melons in the refrigerator if you are not ready to use them; keep under-ripe melons at room temperature to mature. Once cut open, melons should be refrigerated.

Mango purée surrounded by an apple,
a persimmon, and blueberries

Forcing ripening. You can speed up the ripening process for many fruits by simply putting them in a paper bag and leaving them on the counter for a day or two. Gasses released within the bag can trigger faster ripening. Unfortunately, fruits and vegetables picked too early will never ripen properly. Some can be salvaged in juices with the addition of other juices or a dollop of honey or sugar.

Whether you're buying pears, figs, or tomatoes, try to select fruit that has been picked at a mature enough stage to ripen properly.

Using frozen fruits. When good berries are impossible to get or are absurdly expensive, common types of berries are available in the freezer section of the supermarket. Or plan ahead and freeze fresh berries and other ingredients when they are in season for use later in juices and smoothies. Each fruit and vegetable freezes differently, and not always successfully. If you have an overabundance of a particular fruit or vegetable and you want to freeze it, check a large reference cookbook for detailed instructions and advice.

Add dried fruits to enhance flavors. Apricots, raisins, prunes, dates, figs, and other dried fruits are packed with flavor and greatly enhance many fruit juices. To blend them, add into a ½ cup (120 ml) or so of liquid and process until they are the desired consistency. A word of caution: Go easy on herbs; they pack a lot of flavor.

Preserves make good sweeteners. Sometimes all a good but uninteresting glass of juice needs is a dollop of jam, orange marmalade, or preserves to make it special. Add it to the blender as you mix, and remember that you don't need much to enhance the flavor.

Berries hold their flavor better than most frozen fruit. Dried apricots and other dried fruit can add a sweet jolt to dull fruit drinks.

Supplements

Healthy supplements add punch to your drinks.
Supplements like bee pollen, brewer's yeast, spirulina, and various forms of algae—all available in health food stores—are popular additives for boosting nutrients and the protein levels of all kinds of foods. While some have little flavor, others can be difficult for even enthusiasts to swallow. But mixed into a smoothie they all go down without complaint. Experiment on your own and discover which smoothies work best with your favorite additives.

A variety of nutritional supplements can be purchased at the health foods store or in the health foods section of the supermarket.

Resource Guide

Juicer Manufacturers

Acme Juicer Mfg. Co.
Waring Products Division
283 Main Street
New Hartford, CT 06057
Ph: 860.379.0732
Fax: 860.738.0249

The Champion Juicer
Plastaket Manufacturing Company
6220 East Highway 12
Lodi, CA 95240
Ph: 209.369.4638
Fax: 209.369.7455

The Juiceman
Salton Manufacturing
P.O. Box 473
Louisiana, MO 63353
1.800.800.8455

Miracle Juicers
Hans G. Iafors
Evergreen of Sweden
P.O. Box 11061-1061
Springfield, MO 65808
Web: www.littlebigmall.com/
miracle.htm

Omega Products, Inc.
6291 Lyters Lane
P.O. Box 4523
Harrisburg, PA 17111
Ph: 1.800.633.3401
Fax: 717.561.1298

Distributors

Reach4Life Enterprises
Web: www.reach4life.com
carries Acme, Champion, Green-Power, Juiceman, Omega, and a variety of citrus juicers

T J Plus
5631 East Morning Star Road
Cave Creek, AZ 85331
Ph: 602.488.7808
Web: juicebars.clever.net/juicers/
phoenix.htm
carries Acme, Champion, Green-Power, Juiceman, Miracle, and Omega

Index